Dear Parent:
Your child's love of reading starts here!

Every child learns to read in a different way and at his or her own speed. Some go back and forth between reading levels and read favorite books again and again. Others read through each level in order. You can help your young reader improve and become more confident by encouraging his or her own interests and abilities. From books your child reads with you to the first books he or she reads alone, there are I Can Read Books for every stage of reading:

SHARED READING
Basic language, word repetition, and whimsical illustrations, ideal for sharing with your emergent reader

BEGINNING READING
Short sentences, familiar words, and simple concepts for children eager to read on their own

READING WITH HELP
Engaging stories, longer sentences, and language play for developing readers

READING ALONE
Complex plots, challenging vocabulary, and high-interest topics for the independent reader

ADVANCED READING
Short paragraphs, chapters, and exciting themes for the perfect bridge to chapter books

I Can Read Books have introduced children to the joy of reading since 1957. Featuring award-winning authors and illustrators and a fabulous cast of beloved characters, I Can Read Books set the standard for beginning readers.

A lifetime of discovery begins with the magical words "I Can Read!"

Visit www.icanread.com for information
on enriching your child's reading experience.

For Poppy

I Can Read Book® is a trademark of HarperCollins Publishers.
Balzer + Bray is an imprint of HarperCollins Publishers.
Otter: Let's Go Swimming!
www.icanread.com

Library of Congress Control Number: 2016950536
ISBN 978-0-06-236663-4 (paperback) — ISBN 978-0-06-236664-1 (hardcover)

17 18 19 20 21 SCP 10 9 8 7 6 5 4 3 2 1
❖
First Edition

OTTER
Let's Go Swimming!

By SAM GARTON

BALZER + BRAY

An Imprint of HarperCollinsPublishers

Today we go to the beach.

I am so excited!

I will learn to swim in the sea.

I think I will be a very good swimmer.

I have all my swimming
things.

Let's go swimming!

Otter Keeper goes first.

Now it is my turn.

Oh no!
I cannot go swimming now.

Giraffe is scared of fish.

Do not worry, Giraffe.

We will make a sand castle.

"Fish are friendly," says Otter
Keeper.

Okay, but I cannot go swimming now.

Teddy does not like to get wet.

Do not worry, Teddy.

We can play ball.

"Getting wet is fun,"
says Otter Keeper.

Okay, but I cannot go
swimming now.

I am scared of the sea!

I am going to hide.

Otter Keeper says he has
an idea.

Oh no! Now I have to go
swimming.

Everyone is having fun
without me!

Otter Keeper helps me swim.

I kick a lot.

I splash a lot.

I am swimming!

Swimming is not scary.
Swimming is fun!

It is time to go home.

Oh no! We cannot go
home now.

Swimming is too much fun!